CORRECTION
On page 8, the word NORWAY in line two should read DENMARK.

Keith Lye
General Editor
Henry Pluckrose

Franklin Watts
London   New York   Sydney   Toronto

Facts about Denmark

Area:
43,069 sq. km.
(16,629 sq. miles)

Population:
5,153,000 (1984 estimate)

Capital:
Copenhagen

Largest cities:
Copenhagen (population with suburbs, 1,377,000); Aarhus (247,000); Odense (170,000); Aalborg (154,000)

Official language:
Danish

Religion:
Christianity (Lutheran Church)

Main exports:
Machinery and equipment, live animals and meat, dairy products and eggs

Currency:
Krone

Franklin Watts Limited
12a Golden Square
London W1

ISBN: UK Edition 0 86313 212 X
ISBN: US Edition 0 531 04884 5
Library of Congress Catalog
Card No: 84–51507

© Franklin Watts Limited 1984

Typeset by Ace Filmsetting Ltd,
Frome, Somerset
Printed in Hong Kong

Text Editor: Brenda Williams

Maps: Edward Kinsey

Design: Edward Kinsey

Stamps: Stanley Gibbons Limited

Photographs: Danish Tourist Board;
Zefa, 3, 4, 5, 6, 7, 14, 16, 17, 18, 30, 31;
Danish Dairy Board, 15
Front cover: Zefa
Back cover: Danish Tourist Board

The Kingdom of Denmark is a small country in northern Europe. The part named Jutland (Jylland in Danish) is a finger-like area of land, called a peninsula. Jutland is joined to Germany and faces the North Sea in the west. The rest of Denmark is made up of islands.

Denmark includes nearly 500 islands, but only about 100 of these have people living on them. This is the resort of Sandvig, on the island of Bornholm in the Baltic Sea. Most of the islands lie between Jutland and the coast of Sweden.

The largest island is Zealand (Sjælland in Danish) which has much fertile farmland. It is separated from Sweden by a narrow strip of sea called the Sound. Denmark is a low-lying country. Its highest point is only 173 m (568 ft).

Denmark is a monarchy. Since 1972 its monarch has been Queen Margrethe II, who lives at the Amalienborg Palace in Copenhagen. On duty outside the palace is the Royal Guard. Copenhagen (København in Danish) is Denmark's capital city. It stands on the northeast coast of Zealand.

In the heart of Copenhagen is the large Christiansborg Palace. Here the country's laws are made by the Danish parliament, which is called the Folketing. In front of the palace is a smaller building with a spire of dragon's tails. This is the Stock Exchange.

The picture shows some stamps and money used in Norway. The main unit of currency is the krone, which contains 100 ore.

From ancient times, the Danes have been daring sea-farers. Between the 8th and 11th centuries, Danish Vikings raided many parts of Europe. Now each year the people of Frederikssund, on Zealand, hold a Viking festival and act plays based on Viking legends.

The Vikings sailed in longships, like this one in the Viking Ships Museum at Roskilde on Zealand. In the 11th century, Danish Vikings conquered England. Sweyn Forkbeard and his son, Canute, were kings of both Denmark and England.

Most Danes belong to the Lutheran Church. The cathedral at Aarhus (Århus in Danish) is the longest church in the country and one of the finest. Aarhus is on the east coast of Jutland. It is Denmark's second largest city.

Denmark's fourth largest city is Aalborg (or Ålborg) in northern Jutland. It has pretty twisting lanes lined with old houses. About 85 out of every 100 Danes live in cities and towns.

This statue of Hans Christian Andersen (1805–75), Denmark's most famous writer, is in Copenhagen. His fairy tales are still read by people all over the world.

Hans Christian Andersen was born in Odense, Denmark's third largest city, on the island of Fyn. In summer, the children of Odense perform plays based on Andersen's stories.

One of Andersen's fairy tales tells the story of the Little Mermaid. A famous bronze statue of her sits off the shore of Copenhagen. She is looking out to sea, watching the ships at anchor.

Also in Copenhagen are the Tivoli Gardens, open from May to September. Here there is entertainment for all the family, with a funfair and musical concerts. In the evening the buildings are brightly lit and sometimes there are firework displays.

Kronborg Castle in Elsinore (Helsingør in Danish) also attracts visitors. Here the English play *Hamlet*, by William Shakespeare, is sometimes performed. It tells the story of a Prince of Denmark who lived at the castle, on the northeast corner of Zealand.

Dairy produce and meat, including bacon, are also leading products. As farming is so important in Denmark, country shows are popular events. Seven out of every 100 Danes work in farming, forestry and fishing.

Almost three-quarters of Denmark's land is farmed. Leading crops include barley, potatoes, sugar beet and wheat. Other plants are also grown to feed farm animals.

Denmark's largest fishing port is Esbjerg, on the west coast of Jutland. The Danes fish in the North Sea, the Baltic Sea, and the waterways between Denmark, Norway and Sweden.

Denmark is an important industrial country. About 35 out of every 100 workers have jobs in industry. Many industries help to process farm products. Here, rounds of Danish Blue cheese are stored in racks until they are ready for eating.

Danish silverware, shown here, and china are world famous. Denmark is known for its skilled crafts and its modern designs. The Danes also make electrical goods, machinery, transport equipment and other factory products.

23

Many Danish children go to nursery schools. All the country's children must be educated for nine years. The Folkeskolen (folk schools) are free, but there are also some private schools.

These children are enjoying a snack while on a school outing. Many Danes (like other North Europeans such as Finns, Norwegians and Swedes) have fair hair and blue eyes.

Denmark is one of Europe's most wealthy countries. The Danes have a high standard of living and many families own summer cottages. There they can relax, far from the bustle and noise of the cities.

Families enjoy seaside holidays. This picture was taken in the holiday area of Djursland, in eastern Jutland. Summer temperatures in Denmark are about 17°C (63°F). About 550–650 mm (22–26 in) of rain falls in a year.

Many Danes enjoy sailing, as here in the "Round Zealand" regatta. Some boats have skilled crews, but families also enter this event. Swimming and fishing are popular pastimes, but soccer is the national sport.

The Danes wear national costumes at festivals. They are proud of their long history. Denmark's flag has a white cross on a red banner. It has been in use since 1219 – longer than any other country's national flag.

The Faeroe Islands are in the North Atlantic Ocean, between Scotland and Iceland. These Danish islands have their own government. They cover 1,399 sq. km. (540 sq. miles). Most of the 45,000 people depend on fishing for their living.

Greenland is the world's largest island. It, too, is Danish, but has had its own parliament since 1979. Greenland covers 2,175,600 sq. km. (840,004 sq. miles). Most Greenlanders live by fishing. The catch in this picture will be used to make pet food.

Index

Aalborg 13
Aarhus 12
Amalienborg Palace 6
Andersen, Hans Christian
   14–16

Bornholm 4

Cheese 22
Christiansborg Palace 7
Climate 27
Copenhagen 6–7, 14,
   16–17

Djursland 27

Education 24
Elsinore 18
Esbjerg 21

Faeroe Islands 30
Farming 19–20
Fishing 21, 30–31
Flag 29
Frederikssund 10

Government 6–7
Greenland 31

Industries 22–23

Jutland 3, 12–13, 21, 27

Kronborg Castle 18

Little Mermaid 16

Money 8

National costumes 29

Odense 15

Parliament 7
Pastimes 28

Religion 12
Roskilde 11

Sailing 28
Sandvig 4
Schools 24
Silverware 23
Stamps 8
Stock Exchange 7

Tivoli Gardens 17

Vikings 10–11

Zealand 5–6, 10–11, 18, 28